THE 100+ SERIES™
Reproducible Activities

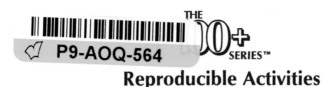

Using the Standards

Problem Solving

Grade 2

By
P. A. M. Howard

Published by Instructional Fair • TS Denison
an imprint of

McGraw Hill Children's Publishing

Author: P. A. M. Howard
Editors: Sara Bierling, Melissa Warner Hale

 **Children's Publishing**

Published by Instructional Fair • TS Denison
An imprint of McGraw-Hill Children's Publishing
Copyright © 2003 McGraw-Hill Children's Publishing

Send all inquiries to:
McGraw-Hill Children's Publishing
3195 Wilson Drive NW
Grand Rapids, Michigan 49544

Using the Standards: Problem Solving—grade 2
ISBN: 0-7424-1822-7

1 2 3 4 5 6 7 8 9 PHXBK 08 07 06 05 04 03

Table of Contents

© McGraw-Hill Children's Publishing

0-7424-1822-7 *Problem Solving*

Introduction

This book is designed around the standards from the National Council of Teachers of Mathematics (NCTM) with a focus on problem solving. Students will build new mathematical knowledge, solve problems in context, apply and adapt appropriate strategies, and reflect on the problem-solving process. At the same time, students will utilize skills from the NCTM content standards:

- Number and Operations
- Algebra
- Geometry
- Measurement
- Data Analysis and Probability

The NCTM process standards are also incorporated throughout the activities. The correlation chart on page 6 identifies the pages on which each NCTM standard appears. Also look for the following process icons on each page:

 Problem Solving   Communication   Reasoning and Proof

 Connections   Representation

Problem-Solving Challenge: This short pretest contains a representative sampling of problem-solving activities similar to those used throughout this book. Give this pretest all at one time, or present one problem at a time over a series of days. Teachers may choose to assign these problems to individuals, pairs, or groups.

The purpose of the pretest is to provide insights into the thought processes and strategies students already possess. The emphasis should not be on the number of "right" answers. Instead encourage students to try their best and write down their ideas. These problems can also provide opportunities for class discussion as students share their thought processes with one another.

0-7424-1822-7 *Problem Solving*

Introduction (cont.)

Workbook Pages: These activities can be done independently, in pairs, or in groups. Since the emphasis is on problem solving rather than computation, calculators may be used to complete some activities.

Many activities will lead into subjects that could be investigated or discussed further as a class. Compare different solution methods or discuss how to select a valid solution method for a particular problem.

Communication: Each activity ends with a communication section. These questions may be used as journal prompts, writing activities, or discussion prompts. Each communication question is labeled **Think** or **Do More**.

Create Your Own Problems: These sections provide students with opportunities to create problems like those they worked on within each content section. Students are given open-ended instructions and asked to share their problems with classmates.

Check Your Skills: These activities provide a representative sample of the types of problems developed throughout each content section. This can be used as additional practice or as a post test.

Cumulative Post Test: This is a short post test providing a representative sample of problems used throughout the book. It may be used for assessment or extra practice. The test can be given all at one time or may be split up over several periods.

Vocabulary Cards: Use the vocabulary cards to familiarize students with mathematical language. The pages may be copied, cut, and glued onto index cards. Glue the front and back on the same index card to make flash cards. Or glue each side on a separate card to use in matching games and activities.

© McGraw-Hill Children's Publishing 0-7424-1822-7 *Problem Solving*

NCTM Standards Correlation Chart

		Problem Solving	Reasoning and Proof	Connections	Representation
Numbers & Operations	number systems	9, 10	14, 15	13, 32	16, 17
	operations	18, 19		20, 21, 24, 25, 26, 36, 37, 40	
	computations & estimation			11, 12, 61, 69, 82	22, 23
Algebra	patterns, relations, & functions	35		32	30, 31, 34
	situations & structures; symbols	38, 39	41	40	
	mathematical models		44, 45	36, 37	36, 37
	change in context			42, 43	
Geometry	properties of two- & three-dimensional shapes	53	52, 54, 55	61	50, 51
	coordinate geometry	63, 64			
	transformations & symmetry	58	56, 67		
	visualization, spatial reasoning, & geometric modeling				49, 59, 60, 62
Measurement	units, systems, & processes of measurement	80, 81		68, 70, 71, 75, 78, 81	73
	techniques, tools, & formulas	74	79	69, 71, 76, 82, 83	72, 77
Data Analysis & Probability	collect, organize, & display data	89, 98		87, 88, 91, 92	87, 88, 90, 93, 94, 95, 99
	statistical methods to analyze data			97, 100	95, 97
	data inferences and predictions			96	93, 96
	basic concepts of probability		101, 102	13	

*All pages are problem solving. Pages listed as problem solving in the chart are those that do not also contain one of the other three process strands.

**The Problem Solving Challenge, Create Your Own Problems, Check Your Skills, and Cumulative Post Test pages are not included on this chart but contain a representative sampling of all content and process standards.

The NCTM communication process strand is found at the end of each activity.

Problem-Solving Challenge

1. There are 5,234 people with tickets to the skating championships.

Write this number in expanded form.

_____

2. Make these equations true by putting in the correct operation (**+**, **−**).

  a. 22 _____ 2 = 24

  b. 26 _____ 2 = 24

  c. 12 _____ 12 = 24

3. Draw a pizza and divide it into 4 equal parts.

What is the fraction for one piece? _____

4. Draw one 2-D shape. Write its name.

5. Draw one 3-D shape. Write its name.

0-7424-1822-7 *Problem Solving*

Problem-Solving Challenge (cont.)

6. Write the unit you would use to measure. Write **inches**, **feet**, or **yards**. Use each once.

a. length of a hallway _____

b. length of your hand _____

c. length of a football field _____

7. Draw a pictograph. Use the information below.

Number of 100% Tests

Week 1—12 tests

Week 2—14 tests

Week 3—17 tests

Week 4—20 tests

Do you see a pattern? What is it?

_____

_____

_____

_____

Name _____ Date _____

Place Value

Directions: Answer each question. Use what you know about place value.

1. Frank was taking $1,678.00 to the bank. Only $1,078.00 was put into the bank. How much was lost? _____

   Write the amount in words. _____

2. **a.** Find the mystery number. This number is the age of a turtle at the zoo. Turtles live to be very old. This turtle's age is equal to 1,171 minus the thousands place. Also subtract the hundreds place.

   How old is the turtle? _____

   b. Write the turtle's age in expanded form. Break up the number by place values.

   _____

   c. How did you find the answer for **b**?

   _____

   _____

3. **a.** Find the mystery number. It is the largest 4-digit number you can make from these numbers: 2, 5, 9, and 1. What is the number? _____

   b. Write the number in expanded form.

   _____

   c. Write the number in words.

   _____

Do More

Compare these 2 numbers: 5,145 and 5,415.
What is the same and what is different?

9

   0-7424-1822-7 *Problem Solving*

Name _____ Date _____

Number Combinations

I. Make 10 numbers greater than 100. Use these numerals: 2, 3, 4, 5, 6, 7, and 8. One has been done for you.

a. ___678___

b. _____

c. _____

d. _____

e. _____

f. _____

g. _____

h. _____

i. _____

j. _____

2. What is the biggest number you can make from the numbers 1, 3, 5, and 9?

_____

How did you solve this problem?

_____

_____

3. What is the smallest number you can make from the numbers 9, 7, 3, and 5?

_____

What plan did you use to find the answer?

_____

_____

Do More

 Make up two questions like those above. Have a classmate answer them.

0-7424-1822-7 *Problem Solving*

Name _____ Date _____

Rounding Numbers

Use with page 12.

Directions: Numbers that end in 0–4 round down. Numbers that end in 5–9 round up. Round to solve the problems below.

1. Round these numbers to the nearest ten. The first one is done for you.

   a. 134 ➔ ___130___   **e.** 16 ➔ _____

   b. 53 ➔ _____   **f.** 71 ➔ _____

   c. 69 ➔ _____   **g.** 36 ➔ _____

   d. 78 ➔ _____   **h.** 25 ➔ _____

2. Round these numbers to the nearest hundred. The first one is done for you.

   a. 102 ➔ ___100___   **e.** 534 ➔ _____

   b. 99 ➔ _____   **f.** 255 ➔ _____

   c. 233 ➔ _____   **g.** 321 ➔ _____

   d. 777 ➔ _____   **h.** 365 ➔ _____

3. Martha's mom wanted to make clothes for Martha. She thought it would cost less than buying them in the stores. Round the cost of clothes at the store to the nearest dollar.

Martha Needs	Store Cost	Rounded Cost
1 skirt	$19.95	_____
1 shirt	$16.95	_____
1 pair of jeans	$39.00	_____
1 T-shirt	$9.95	_____

4. Look at the rounded prices. How much would all the clothes cost? _____

   How much would they cost exactly? _____

   What is the difference between the two totals? _____

11

Rounding Numbers (cont.)

Use with page 11.

5. Martha's mom can get all the material she needs for $39.75.
Round this cost to the nearest dollar. _____

How did you know how to round?

_____

_____

6. She will need to buy 4 spools of thread for $2.29 each.
How much will that be? _____

Round this cost to the nearest dollar. _____

7. How much will all the supplies cost in rounded dollars?
Show how you got your answer. _____

8. How much will all the supplies cost in actual dollars and cents? _____

9. Compare the difference in cost in rounded dollars between buying the clothes
at a store or making them at home (see p. 11).

_____

10. Would you buy the clothes or make them. Why?

_____

_____

Think

What do you think about rounding prices or numbers to make a guess?
How might this be helpful? When would it not be a good idea?

0-7424-1822-7 *Problem Solving*

Name _____ Date _____

Putting Numbers Together

1. a. Joe forgot the combination to his locker. He knows there are 3 numbers: 3, 5, and 8. How many combinations can there be? Write them below.

_____   _____   _____

_____   _____   _____

b. How did you find the answer?

_____

_____

2. Terry, his sisters Norma and Jean, and his mom and dad are going for a ride in the country. They can't agree about who will sit where in the car. Dad has to drive, since Terry's mom broke her foot. Mom will sit in the front. How many different ways can they sit? _____

3. a. Think of a number: _____

b. Double it: _____

c. Add 10 to it: _____

d. Cut it in half: _____

e. Take away your original number: _____

f. If your answer is 5, you got it right.

Think

Why does the magic number combination (problem 3) work?

0-7424-1822-7 *Problem Solving*

Adding Odd and Even

Directions: An odd number cannot be divided into 2 equal groups. Even numbers can be divided into 2 equal groups. If a number ends in an odd number, it is odd. If a number ends in an even number, it is even. Use what you know about odd and even numbers to complete the problems below.

1. a. What will happen when you add two even numbers?
Answer these problems to see what happens.

$$\begin{array}{cccc} 4 & 22 & 44 & 2{,}322 \\ +\ 6 & +\ 64 & +\ 32 & +\ 1{,}214 \end{array}$$

    b. Were the answers to these problems odd or even?

_____

2. a. What will happen when you add two odd numbers?
Answer these problems to see what happens.

$$\begin{array}{cccc} 137 & 13 & 49 & 2{,}133 \\ +\ 523 & +\ 19 & +\ 51 & +\ 4{,}001 \end{array}$$

    b. Were the answers to these problems odd or even?

_____

3. a. What will happen when you add an odd and an even number together?
Answer these questions to see what happens.

$$\begin{array}{cccc} 45 & 13 & 127 & 653 \\ +\ 22 & +\ 20 & +\ 444 & +\ 522 \end{array}$$

    b. Were the answers to these problems odd or even?

_____

Think

Why do these problems have the same kind of sum each time?

14

0-7424-1822-7 *Problem Solving*

Name _____ Date _____

Subtracting Odd and Even

Directions: Use what you know about odd and even numbers to solve the following problems.

1. Subtract these sets of even numbers. What will the answers tell you?

6	10	12	2,322
− 4	− 4	− 6	− 1,214

2. Subtract these sets of odd numbers. What will the answers tell you?

7	9	133	2,977
− 5	− 3	− 11	− 1,357

3. Subtract these numbers. You will take an odd number from an even number. What will the answers tell you?

16	56	288	2,466
− 11	− 31	− 151	− 1,111

4. What results were found after working with odd and even numbers when subtracting?

_____

_____

Think

How good were your guesses?
What did you use to help you make a guess?

0-7424-1822-7 *Problem Solving*

Name _____ Date _____

Fractions

Directions: Use what you know about fractions to solve the problems.

1. This is a whole orange. Divide the orange in half. Make 2 equal parts. Write the correct fraction on each equal part.

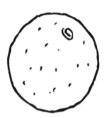

2. The pizza below has been divided into 4 equal parts. Write the correct fraction in each part.

3. Color 2 of the 4 pizza pieces above red.
     What fraction of the pizza did you color? _____

4. How do you know your answer to #3 is correct?

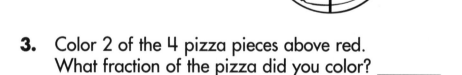

5. How much of the pizza is not colored? _____

Do More

Write a number sentence that will show what happened in the pizza problem.

0-7424-1822-7 *Problem Solving*

Name _____ Date _____

Fraction Bars

This picture shows whole bars divided into a different number of parts. All the parts together make 1 whole bar.

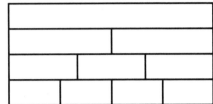

1. The top bar is a whole bar. Write this name on it.

2. The second bar is in two equal parts. Both parts are called $\frac{1}{2}$. Write this fraction on both parts.

3. How many parts does the third bar have? _____ Write the correct fraction name on each part.

4. How many parts does the fourth bar have? _____ Write the correct fraction name on each part.

5. **a.** Which is a larger piece— $\frac{1}{4}$ or $\frac{1}{3}$?

   b. Which is a larger piece— $\frac{1}{2}$ or $\frac{1}{3}$?

   c. Which one is equal to $\frac{2}{4}$? _____

   How do you know your answer is correct?

_____

Think

What do the top and bottom numbers of a fraction mean?

0-7424-1822-7 *Problem Solving*

Name _____ Date _____

Choose Your Operation

1. Choose the math signs (**+** or **−**) needed to make these number sentences true.

   a. 33 ___ 5 ___ 15 = 53

   b. 14 ___ 2 ___ 1 = 17

   c. 25 ___ 2 = 16 ___ 7

   d. 8 ___ 8 ___ 4 = 4

   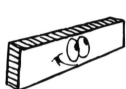
   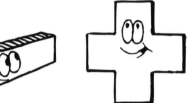

2. Write four number sentences with operation signs missing. Have a classmate solve them.

   _____

   _____

   _____

   _____

3. Make 4 different number sentences equal to 12. Use addition (**+**) and subtraction (**−**).

   _____

   _____

   _____

   _____

Do More

Tell how you wrote one of your problems for #3.

18

0-7424-1822-7 *Problem Solving*

Name _____ Date _____

Missing Numbers

Directions: Find the missing numbers. Sometimes more than one answer is correct.

1. **a.** _____ + _____ = 12

    b. _____ − 4 = 14

    c. 8 + _____ + _____ = 26

    d. 16 − _____ + _____ = 9

    e. 10 + _____ = 4 + _____

    f. _____ + _____ = 22 − _____

2. How did you find the answer for **c**?

    _____

    _____

3. What was the hardest part of solving these problems?

    _____

    _____

Do More

Write four number sentences with missing numbers. Have the missing numbers in different spots. Have a classmate solve the number sentences.

0-7424-1822-7 *Problem Solving*

Name _____ Date _____

Groups and Pairs

Directions: Solve each problem. Draw pictures to help you.

1. How many people would there be if you had a total of 200 fingers and toes? Show how you found your answer.

2. How many chairs (4 legs) and stools (2 legs) might there be if there are a total of 78 legs?

What is most difficult about this problem?

_____

_____

3. How many horses (4 legs) and chickens (2 legs) are in the barn if you count 42 feet? Find 2 ways to solve.

Do More

Write one of your own combination problems.

0-7424-1822-7 *Problem Solving*

Name _____ Date _____

Calendar Calculations

1. There are 7 days in 1 week. How many days are there in 10 weeks? _____

What operation did you use to find your answer? _____

7 days = 1 week
4 weeks = 1 month
12 months = 1 year
52 weeks = 1 year
365 days = 1 year

2. There are 52 weeks in 1 year. How many weeks will have passed by your seventh birthday? _____

Show how you found your answer.

3. If the tree you planted is 5 years old. How many days has it been living? _____

Using words, tell how you found the answer.

_____

_____

_____

_____

Do More

Compare your age to a dog the same age in human years. There are about seven dog years to one human year. How much "older" would the dog be?

0-7424-1822-7 *Problem Solving*

Name _____ Date _____

Find the Sums

1. Place 3 numbers in each section of each triangle. The sum of the 3 numbers must equal the number in the middle.

a. 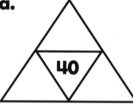   b.    c.    d.

2. Place 4 numbers in each section of each rectangle. The sum of the numbers in the squares must equal the number in the middle.

a. 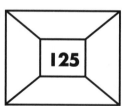   b. 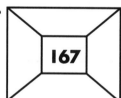   c. 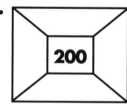   d.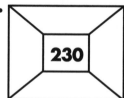

Do More

Explain how you found numbers to get the correct answers.

0-7424-1822-7 *Problem Solving*

Name _____ Date _____

Making Change

1. Gavin gave the storekeeper $1.00 for a comic book costing $0.45. Draw the change he should get back. Show your answer in two different ways.

2. Peter has 18 nickels saved to buy a toy car that costs $3.00. How much more does he need? Show how you found your answer.

3. What is the most a set of 4 coins can be worth if each coin in the set is a different value? Choose from half-dollar, quarter, dime, nickel, and penny. How did you find your answer?

Do More

Use groups of pennies to show the value of a nickel, a dime, and a quarter.

0-7424-1822-7 *Problem Solving*

Name _____ Date _____

Divide It Up

1. Justin forgot his lunch at home. His friend David shared his lunch with him. David had 1 sandwich, 24 grapes, 6 cookies, and an 8-ounce carton of milk. Divide David's lunch so that they both get the same amount. Describe how you divided the lunch.

_____

_____

_____

_____

2. Old MacDonald has a farm. Many people leave their animals at his farm. MacDonald is outside one morning scratching his head. He knows he has too many animals.

   a. He owns only 12 chickens. Now he has half as many more. How many chickens are there now? _____

   b. He has double the number of horses, which is usually 18. How many horses are not his? _____

   c. Suggest some ways you could have found the answer.

   _____

   _____

Think

What do **half as many more** and **double** mean?

0-7424-1822-7 *Problem Solving*

5-Step Problem Solving

Use with page 26.

The 5-Step Problem Solving Formula:

1. Find the question. Circle it.
2. Reread the problem. Find things you don't need to use to solve. Cross them out gently (you may need them later).
3. Underline the important information.
4. Find the words that tell you what operation to use. Circle them.
5. Solve the problem.

Problem 1:

Ken plays on a soccer team. The team is all boys who are 8 years old. The team has 16 players. The team uniform is blue and white. Ken scored 18 goals in September, 23 goals in October, and 25 goals in November. How many goals did he score in all?

Step 1: What is the question you are being asked to solve? Circle it and write it here.

Step 2: Reread the problem. Cross out information you don't need. Cross out gently with a pencil. You may need the information later. List the unneeded information here.

Step 3: Underline the important information and list it here.

Step 4: Find the words in the problem that help you know what operation you need to use. Circle them. Write the words here.

Step 5: Solve the problem.

0-7424-1822-7 *Problem Solving*

Name _____ Date _____

5-Step Problem Solving (cont.)

Use with page 25.

Problem 2:

Ivan is 7 and in second grade. There are 26 students in his class. Half are girls and half are boys. Ivan's mom bought him a new jumbo box of crayons for school. The box of crayons had enough crayons to use a different color every day for 2 months. How many crayons were in the box?

Step 1: What is the question? Circle it but do not write it here.

Step 2: Reread the problem and cross out any information you don't need. Why do you think this information is there?

Step 3: Underline the important information. Do not list it here.

Step 4: Find the words that help you know what operation you need to use. Circle them. How do you know what the words are telling you to do?

Step 5: Solve the problem. Show your work.

Think

What was the most difficult step of problem 2?

0-7424-1822-7 *Problem Solving*

Name _____   Date _____

Create Your Own Problems

1. Write a word problem that uses rounding up or down. This should be a real-life problem.

2. Design a 5-step problem. Use school as a theme. Make sure the problem contains information not needed to solve.

3. Write a number riddle. Use place-value words. The answer should be written in standard form, expanded form, and written form.

4. Create a real-life problem using $\frac{1}{2}$, $\frac{1}{3}$, or $\frac{1}{4}$.

0-7424-1822-7 *Problem Solving*

Name _____ Date _____

Check Your Skills

1. There are 3,598 people who come to Walker's Creek for the summer.

Write this number in expanded form. _____

Write this number in written form. _____

2. Of all the people in Walker's Creek, $\frac{1}{2}$ are men. How can you find out how many men this is? _____

3. Write the largest four-digit number you can with these numerals: 1, 3, 9, and 8. _____

4. Choose the operation needed to make each math sentence true.

a. 24 _____ 6 = 40 _____ 10

b. 6 _____ 6 _____ 6 = 3 _____ 2 _____ 1

5. Write a number greater than 425. _____

Is the number you wrote even or odd? _____

How do you know? _____

28

0-7424-1822-7 *Problem Solving*

Name _____ Date _____

Check Your Skills (cont.)

6. Write a number less than 145. _____

Is the number you wrote even or odd? _____

How do you know? _____

7. Draw a pizza. Divide it into 4 equal parts.
Label each part with the correct fraction.

_____

8. a. Ted spent $3.59 for lunch. Round this to the nearest dollar. _____

b. Ted paid for his lunch with $4.00. Using the exact cost of his lunch,
not the rounded cost, how much change should Ted get back? Show
how you found your answer. Draw the change.

9. Sherry, who is 8, had a job walking dogs. She got paid $1.00 an hour for
each dog she walked. She usually took them to the off-leash park so they
could run and play. Sherry took 3 dogs at the same time and kept them out
for 1 hour 2 times each day. How much would she make for the day? Use the
5-step formula to solve this problem.

0-7424-1822-7 *Problem Solving*

Name _____ Date _____

Predicting Patterns

Directions: Finish each of the patterns below.

1.

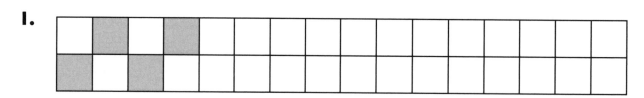

2.

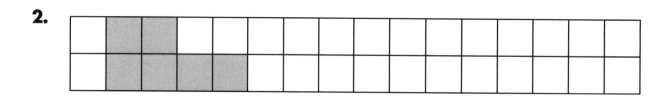

3.

4.

5.

Think

Where do you see patterns every day?

0-7424-1822-7 *Problem Solving*

Name _____ Date _____

Mosaic Tiles

Directions: Become a mosaic artist. Finish the pattern below. Then create a new pattern every three rows.

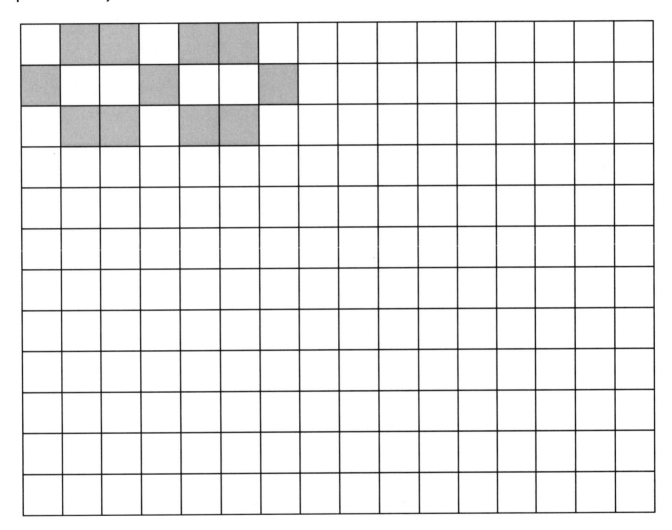

Think

Why do you think artists use patterns?

0-7424-1822-7 *Problem Solving*

Name _____ Date _____

One Hundred Chart

Directions: Use a hundred chart for each problem below.

1. **a.** Skip count by 2s from 2 to 100. Color each number you land on green.

   b. Tell about the pattern you made.

   _____

   c. How many numbers did you color? _____

2. **a.** Skip count by 3s from 3 to 100. Color each number you land on red. If you land on a number already colored green, circle it with red.

   b. How many numbers does counting by 2 share with counting by 3? _____

   c. What is largest number you colored? _____

3. **a.** Skip count by 5s from 5 to 100. Color these numbers blue. If you land on a number already colored or circled, circle it blue, too.

   b. How many of the numbers you landed on were already colored or circled? _____

Think

What is similar about the numbers colored more than one time.

32

0-7424-1822-7 *Problem Solving*

Name _____ Date _____

Patterns with Letters and Numbers

Directions: Look at the letter and number pattern. Use words to tell about the pattern.

1. A1   B2   C3   D4   E5   F6   G7   H8

_____

_____

2. Now continue the pattern. Finish the whole alphabet.

_____

_____

_____

3. Use the pattern above as a code. Write one sentence.
Then write it in the code.

_____

_____

_____

_____

Do More

Write 2 reasons you might want to use a pattern code. Explain how the pattern is important to the code.

0-7424-1822-7 *Problem Solving*

Name _____ Date _____

Flag Patterns

Directions: Look at the United State flag. Find two patterns. Write about the patterns. Then color the flag according to the right patterns.

Pattern 1:

_____

_____

_____

Pattern 2:

_____

_____

_____

Do More

Create your own flag. It must have two patterns. Write what the patterns are.

0-7424-1822-7 *Problem Solving*

Name _____ Date _____

Recognizing Patterns

Directions: Look at each number in each table below. Look for a pattern between the IN and OUT numbers. Use the pattern to fill in the missing numbers.

1.

IN	0	1	2	3	4	5
OUT	2	3	4			

Rule:

2.

IN	0	1	2	3	4	5
OUT	5	6	7			

Rule:

3.

IN	10	9	8	7	6	5
OUT	7	6	5			

Rule:

Do More

Draw your own table. Make up a rule. Trade with a friend.

35

0-7424-1822-7 *Problem Solving*

Addition and Subtraction with Symbols

Directions: Solve the math problems by drawing. Use the pictures shown. The first one is done for you.

1.
$$
\begin{array}{r}
28 \\
-\ 13 \\
\hline
15
\end{array}
$$
○○○○○○○
○○○○○○○
○⊘⊘⊘⊘⊘⊘
⊘⊘⊘⊘⊘⊘⊘

2.
$$
\begin{array}{r}
8 \\
+\ 6 \\
\hline
\end{array}
$$
☆

3.
$$
\begin{array}{r}
14 \\
+\ 9 \\
\hline
\end{array}
$$
■

4.
$$
\begin{array}{r}
31 \\
-\ 12 \\
\hline
\end{array}
$$
♥

Directions: Now write a story problem that uses pictures to solve.

5. _____

_____

_____

_____

Think

What real-life math problems do you solve using pictures or objects?

0-7424-1822-7 *Problem Solving*

Name _____ Date _____

Modeling with Symbols

Directions: Study the drawing below. It represents an equation.

Example: 10 + 15 = 25

✓✓✓✓✓   ✓✓✓✓✓   ✓✓✓✓✓✓✓✓✓✓
✓✓✓✓✓   **+** ✓✓✓✓✓   **=**   ✓✓✓✓✓✓✓✓✓✓
                ✓✓✓✓✓   ✓✓✓✓✓

Directions: Make a drawing for each. Solve the equation.

1. 12 + 14 = _____

2. 15 + 8 = _____

3. 6 + 5 = _____

4. 10 + 6 = _____

Do More

Create a drawing of many objects. Then write a number sentence about your drawing.

0-7424-1822-7 *Problem Solving*

Name _____ Date _____

Using Comparison Signs

>	<	=
greater than	**less than**	**equal to**

Directions: Circle the correct sign.

1. 19   >   <   =   12

2. 35   >   <   =   68

3. 29   >   <   =   72

Directions: Write the correct comparison sign.

4. 13 + 7 [   ] 26 – 4

5. 46 + 3 [   ] 130 – 13

Directions: Write what each sign means.

6. > _____

7. < _____

8. = _____

9. Write a rule to help others remember when to use each sign.

_____

_____

_____

_____

Think

When is it important to know how to compare numbers?

0-7424-1822-7 *Problem Solving*

Name _____ Date _____

Symbolic Notation

Directions: Sometimes we use pictures to talk about numbers. Look at the numbers. Write **>** (greater than), **<** (less than), or **=** (equal) on the line. Then write a sentence about the numbers. The first one has been done for you.

1. 34 $\leq$ 47

34 is less than 47.

2. 98 ____ 89

_____

3. 10 ____ 7

_____

4. 54 ____ 54

_____

5. 298 ____ 297

_____

6. 67 ____ 75

_____

7. 18 ____ 27

_____

8. 143 ____ 134

_____

Do More

Write what **>** (greater than), **<** (less than), and **=** (equal) mean.

0-7424-1822-7 *Problem Solving*

Name _____ Date _____

Properties of Operations

Directions: Fill in the missing numbers to show equal values.

1. $9 + \boxed{} = 10 + 11$

2. $8 + 7 = 9 + \boxed{}$

3. $6 + 5 = 5 + \boxed{}$

4. $\boxed{} + 4 = 5 + 3$

5. $\boxed{} + 1 = 1 + 9$

6. $11 + 11 = 12 + \boxed{}$

Directions: Write 4 problems with missing numbers.

7. _____

8. _____

9. _____

10. _____

Think

When might you need to find a missing number in real life?

0-7424-1822-7 *Problem Solving*

Name _____ Date _____

Working with Zero

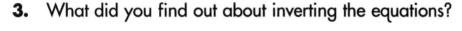

1. Solve these problems.

   a. $9 + 0 =$ **b.** $0 + 9 =$

   c. $21 + 0 =$ **d.** $0 + 21 =$

2. What did you find out about adding with zero?

_____

3. What did you find out about inverting the equations?

For example: $9 + 0 =$ inverts to $0 + 9 =$.

_____

4. Solve these problems. If a problem cannot be solved with positive numbers, write **no** next to it.

   a. $16 - 0 =$ **b.** $0 - 16 =$

   c. $99 - 0 =$ **d.** $0 - 99 =$

   e. $12 - 0 =$ **f.** $0 - 12 =$

5. What did you find out about subtracting with zero?

_____

What did you find out about inverting subtraction equations?

_____

Do More

Find zero written 5 times in your school. What is it showing?

0-7424-1822-7 *Problem Solving*

Name _____ Date _____

Qualitative Change

Directions: Look at how each student grew. Circle the correct word.

1. Renae grew 1 inch in second grade.

   Renae is _____.

   a. shorter   **b.** taller

2. Claudia took off her shoes.

   Claudia is _____.

   a. shorter   **b.** taller

Directions: Read each sentence. Write the correct word on the line.

3. Hannah's hair was 3 feet long. She cut off 2 feet. Hannah's hair is _____.

   Which words told you the answer? _____

4. Jacob weighed 50 pounds in kindergarten. Now Jacob is in second grade. Jacob weighs 62 pounds. Jacob is _____ .

   How do you know? _____

Think

Can you write a comparison sentence about yourself? Have you gotten taller, longer, bigger, or smaller?

0-7424-1822-7 *Problem Solving*

Name _____ Date _____

Quantitative Change

Directions: Look at the graph. Answer the questions.

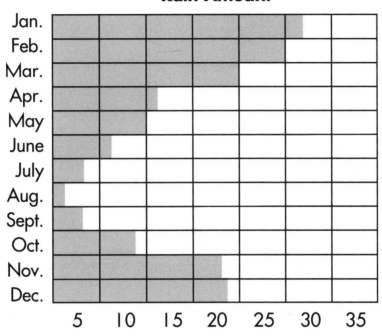

Rain Amount

1. Does the change in rain amounts between Sept. and Oct. get higher or lower?

   _____

2. Between which two months is the highest change?

   _____

3. Write one sentence about how the amount of rain changes.

   _____

Do More

Keep track of the amount of rain that falls in one week. Make a graph.

43

0-7424-1822-7 *Problem Solving*

Name _____ Date _____

Create Some Order

I. Christen is taller than Tommy and older than Zed. Zed isn't as tall as Tommy or as old as Christen. Tommy is younger than both boys.

  a. Draw a picture that will help you organize these boys in order from tallest to shortest.

  b. Draw a picture that will help you organize these boys from the oldest to the youngest.

Think

How did you solve the problem. What would you do differently next time?

0-7424-1822-7 *Problem Solving*

Order It

Mrs. Chin had 3 children. Robert (12), Karen (11), and Michael (9). Each weekend the children had chores to do before they could play. Today Mrs. Chin told one of her children to wash the dishes, one of them to return the books to the library, and one of them to vacuum the house. All the chores were done.

1. Robert did not wash the dishes. Karen did not take the books to the library and Mike did not vacuum. Mike doesn't like to do any kind of cleaning.

Who did what chore?

_____

2. How did you find the answer?

_____

3. Some problems have information that isn't important .

List that information below.

_____

_____

Think

What is one tip you would give a classmate to help solve this problem?

0-7424-1822-7 *Problem Solving*

Create Your Own Problems

1. Use grid paper. Create a mosaic for someone else to complete.

2. Write four problems that have missing numbers. Have a classmate solve them.

a. _____

b. _____

c. _____

d. _____

3. Write four equations using > (greater than), < (less than), and = (equal).

a. _____

b. _____

c. _____

d. _____

4. Make an IN/OUT table. Write numbers under IN. Then create a rule. Fill in the OUT section.

0-7424-1822-7 *Problem Solving*

Algebra

Name _____ Date _____

Check Your Skills

1. Continue the pattern.

    a. ABCD ABCD ABCD A_____

2. Explain the pattern.

A 1 B 2 C 3 D 4 E 5 F 5 G 6 H 7 I 8

_____

3. Complete the charts. Write the rule.

a.

IN	1	2	3	4	5
OUT	0	1	2		

Rule:

b.

IN	1	2	3	4	5
OUT	2	4	6		

Rule:

c.

IN	1	2	3	4	5
OUT	11	12	13		

Rule:

47

0-7424-1822-7 *Problem Solving*

Name _____ Date _____

Check Your Skills (cont.)

4. Draw stars to show this problem. Write the answer.

$15 - 4 =$ _____

5. Write what each sign means.

a. > _____

b. < _____

c. = _____

6. Choose **>**, **<**, or **=** to fill in the box.

a. 24 ☐ 17

b. 3 + 4 ☐ 7 − 0

c. 0 ☐ 0 − 0

d. 135 ☐ 35

7. Fill in the missing numbers.

a. 12 + 9 = 21 − ☐

b. ☐ − 6 = 31 + 8

c. 24 + 25 = 100 − ☐

48

0-7424-1822-7 *Problem Solving*

Name _____ Date _____

Fit It Together

Directions: Cut out the pentomino set (p. 109). Put the pieces together so they make one large rectangle. Trace the pentominoes below to show your solution.

Do More

Use pentominoes to create unusual shapes. Trace to record.

0-7424-1822-7 *Problem Solving*

Name _____ Date _____

Building 2-D Shapes

Directions: Look at each shape name. Match each shape to its name. Draw the shapes that are missing.

1. circle

2. pentagon

3. octagon

4. triangle

5. square

6. hexagon

7. rectangle

8. Which shape was the hardest to draw? Why? _____

_____

Do More

Draw 5 shapes that you see in your classroom.

0-7424-1822-7 *Problem Solving*

Name _____ Date _____

3-D Shapes

Three-dimensional (3-D) shapes have three measurements: length, width, and height. They can have edges, corners, and curves. Look at the pictures of 3-D shapes below. The dotted lines show edges you can't see from the front.

Directions: Match each shape to its name.

1. 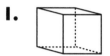   cylinder

2.   cube

3.   prism

4.   cone

5.   sphere

6. Look at these two 3-D shapes. Write 3 things that are alike.

a.    **b.**

_____   _____   _____

7. Draw another 3-D shape.

Do More

Write the definition of a 3-D shape.

0-7424-1822-7 *Problem Solving*

Name _____ Date _____

What Am I?

Directions: Read the clues. Guess the shape. Write the name of the shape on the line. Draw a line to match the clue to the shape.

Shape Names			
cube	rectangle	cylinder	triangle

1. I am a flat shape.
I have 3 points.
I have 3 sides.
What am I? _____
Which clue helped you? _____

2. I am a 3-D shape.
Two faces are circles.
I look like a drinking glass.
What am I? _____
Which clue helped you? _____

3. I am a 3-D shape.
I have 6 sides.
You can use me to play.
You can use me to build things.
What am I? _____
Which clue helped you? _____

4. I am a flat shape.
I have 4 corners.
My sides are not the same length.
What am I? _____
Which clue helped you? _____

Do More

Write 2 shape riddles.

0-7424-1822-7 *Problem Solving*

Name _____ Date _____

Compare and Order

Directions: Put the pictures in order from smallest to largest. Write 1, 2, and 3.

1.

2.

3.

4. Draw 3 circles: one small, one medium, and one large.

5. Draw 3 stars: one small, one medium, and one large.

Think

 How else can you compare and order shapes?

53

0-7424-1822-7 *Problem Solving*

Name _____ Date _____

Group Them

Directions: Look at the groups of shapes. Write the rule used for each group.

Group 1   **Group 2**

_____   _____

_____   _____

_____   _____

_____   _____

Draw another shape for Group 1.   Draw another shape for Group 2.

Do More

Create a Group 3 using a different rule.

0-7424-1822-7 *Problem Solving*

Name _____ Date _____

Same Size, Same Shape

Directions: Shapes that are the same size and the same shape are **congruent**. Use this information to complete the problems.

1. Look at the sets of shapes below. Write **true** beside the ones that are congruent. Write **false** beside the ones that are not.

a. 　　**b.** 　　**c.**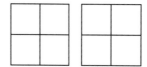

2. How do you know when shapes are not congruent?

_____

_____

3. Draw 2 congruent shapes and 2 shapes that are not congruent. You may trace pattern block shapes to help you.

Do More

　Find congruent and similar shapes in your classroom.

0-7424-1822-7 *Problem Solving*

Name _____ Date _____

Symmetrical Shapes

A shape is **symmetrical** if you can divide it into two parts exactly the same. A line of symmetry divides a shape into two parts exactly the same.

Directions: Are these shapes symmetrical? Circle **YES** or **NO**. The first one has been done for you. How did you know to answer yes or no? Now draw lines of symmetry on the shapes circled yes.

1.

(YES) NO

2.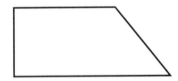

YES NO

3.

YES NO

4.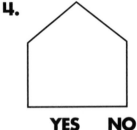

YES NO

5.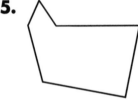

YES NO

6. Draw one shape that is symmetrical. Draw a line of symmetry.

Do More

Draw half of a shape. Tell a friend what symmetry is. Have your friend draw the other half of the shape and make it symmetrical.

0-7424-1822-7 *Problem Solving*

Name _____ Date _____

Complete the Shapes

Directions: Finish these shapes so they are symmetrical. The line of symmetry is drawn for each shape.

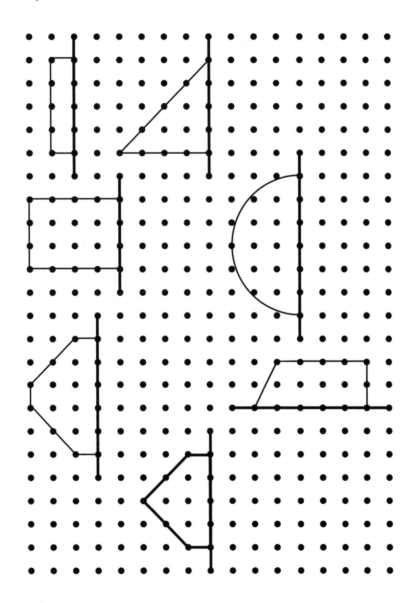

Think

How did the dots above help you draw the other half?

0-7424-1822-7 *Problem Solving*

Name _____ Date _____

Slides, Flips, Turns

Directions: Look at each set of shapes. Circle the slide, flip, or turn.

Slide

1.    **a.**   **b.**   **c.**

Flip

2.   **a.**   **b.**   **c.**

Turn

3.   **a.**   **b.**   **c.**

Directions: Look at each shape. Draw a slide, flip, or turn.

Slide   **Flip**   **Turn**

4.   5.   6.

Think

Where do you see slides, flips, and turns every day?

0-7424-1822-7 *Problem Solving*

Name _____ Date _____

Copying Tangrams

Directions: Your teacher will need to copy the set of tangrams from page 108. Cut out the tangrams. Arrange your tangram pieces to copy these shapes. Trace the tangram pieces onto paper.

duck

fox

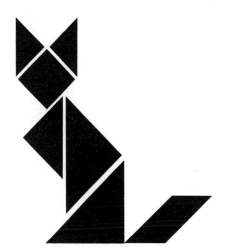

rabbit

Do More

Create a tangram animal of your own.

0-7424-1822-7 *Problem Solving*

Name _____ Date _____

Moving Tangrams

1. Use tangrams to copy this shape.

bear

2. Use tangrams to make a dog. Draw how you did it.

3. Now use tangrams to make a new picture. Draw how you did it.

Do More

Use tangrams to tell a story. Change the placement of the tangrams to create different characters.

0-7424-1822-7 *Problem Solving*

Name _____ Date _____

Finding Perimeter

The **perimeter** is the total distance around a shape. A small shape can be measured in centimeters or inches. To find the perimeter, add all the sides together.

1. Find the perimeters of these 2 shapes. Write the perimeter in the center of each shape.

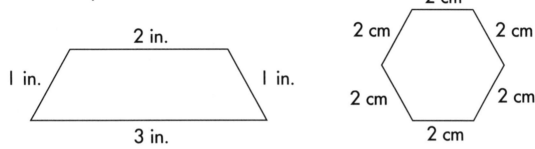

2. How do you find the perimeter of this square if you know how long two sides are? Show your work.

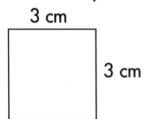

3. Draw a rectangle that has two 3-inch sides and two 2-inch sides. Mark the inches on each side.

Tell how you will find the perimeter. Give the answer.

_____

Think

How is being able to find the perimeter helpful to you outside of school?

0-7424-1822-7 *Problem Solving*

Name _____ Date _____

Position and Location

Directions: The Abeds are staying at Pines Trailer Park. Use the map to help them get around.

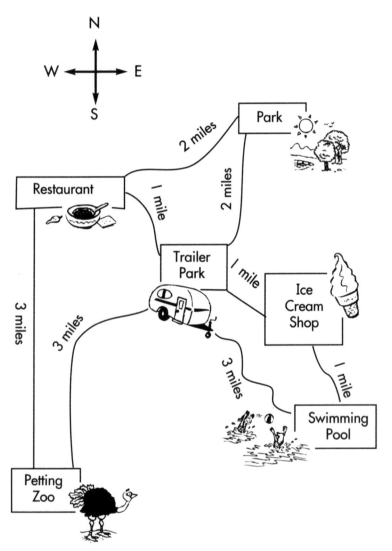

1. Which is farther from the zoo—the park or the swimming pool?

   _____

2. Juna wants to run from the trailer park to the park. Then she will run to the restaurant. How far will she run in all?

   _____

3. Ibrahim is walking south from the trailer park. To which places can he go?

   _____

4. Draw a movie theater on the map. It should be north of the trailer park and closer to the restaurant than the park.

Do More

Draw a map of your school neighborhood.

62

0-7424-1822-7 *Problem Solving*

Name _____ Date _____

Coordinates

Ordered pairs are 2 numbers that tell you how to move on a grid to find a point. The numbers, called coordinates, are always in brackets. The first number tells you how many spaces right to move. The second number tells you how many spaces up to move. These are some coordinates: (1, 2).

Directions: Look at the grid to answer the questions.

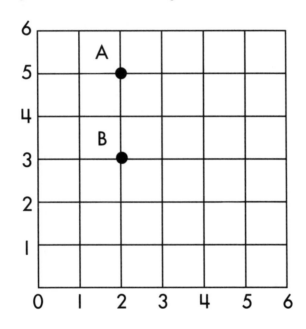

1. What are the coordinates of letter A? _____

2. What letter is at (2, 3)? _____

3. Draw a star at (5, 1).

Do More

Make up grid directions for a classmate to follow.

0-7424-1822-7 *Problem Solving*

Name _____ Date _____

Using Coordinate Grids

Directions: Use the grid and what you know about coordinates. Remember, go right first, then up. Draw a dot at each point. Then connect the dots in order. Connect the first and last dots.

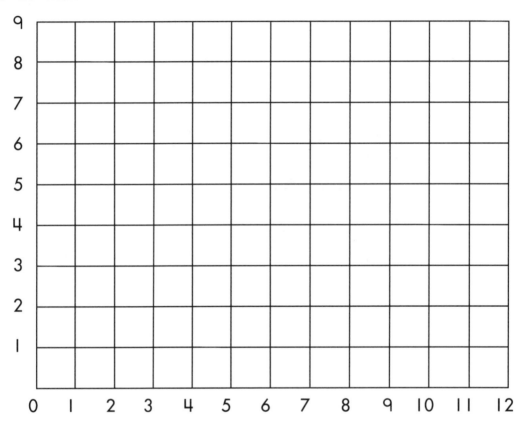

1.	(10, 6)	5.	(7, 5)	9.	(3, 5)	13.	(4, 6)
2.	(10, 4)	6.	(7, 4)	10.	(3, 4)	14.	(4, 7)
3.	(8, 4)	7.	(4, 4)	11.	(2, 4)	15.	(7, 7)
4.	(8, 5)	8.	(4, 5)	12.	(2, 6)	16.	(7, 6)

17. What did you draw? _____ Add details.

Do More

Make up a coordinate drawing. Draw a picture on grid paper. Write down the points. Have a classmate follow the coordinates to make your picture.

0-7424-1822-7 *Problem Solving*

Name _____ Date _____

Create Your Own Problems

1. Create a picture (person, animal, or plant) using tangrams. Challenge a friend to copy it.

2. Write 3 shape riddles. Write about 2-D or 3-D shapes.

3. Use the grid below to draw a picture. Then write down the coordinates. Give the coordinates to a friend to solve.

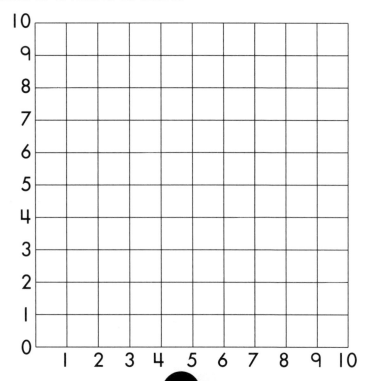

0-7424-1822-7 *Problem Solving*

Name _____ Date _____

Check Your Skills

1. Draw each 2-D shape.

   a. circle   **e.** pentagon

   b. square   **f.** hexagon

   c. rectangle   **g.** octagon

   d. triangle

2. Write the name of each 3-D shape.

   a. _____   **d.** _____

   b. _____   **e.** _____

   c. _____

3. Solve this shape riddle.

   I am a 3-D shape.
   I have 6 sides.
   I have 6 edges.
   All of my sides are the same size.

   What am I? _____

                            0-7424-1822-7 *Problem Solving*

Name _____ Date _____

Check Your Skills (cont.)

4. What does symmetrical mean?

_____

_____

5. What does congruent mean?

_____

_____

6. Draw a triangle. Then flip it.

7. Look at the grid. What is at (2, 5)? _____

Draw a box at (4, 3).

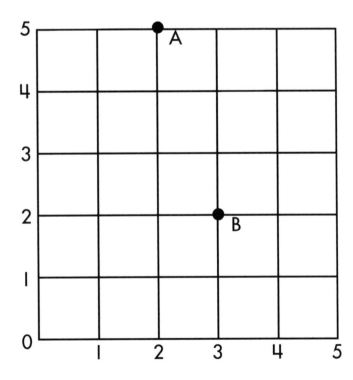

0-7424-1822-7 *Problem Solving*

Name _____ Date _____

In Order

Directions: Estimate the weight of these items from lightest to the heaviest. Write them in the correct order.

1. shoe, sock, glove _____

2. car, horse, bus _____

3. bike, skateboard, in-line skates _____

4. How did you decide the order of the items in 3?

_____

Directions: Estimate how long. Write these sets in order from shortest to longest.

5. your shoe, your hand, your foot _____

6. book, desk, 12-inch ruler_____

Directions: Estimate which holds more. Put them in order from most to least.

7. cup, trash basket, pocket _____

8. cereal box, my desk, my backpack _____

Do More

Find 5 objects in your classroom. Estimate their weights. Then put them in order.

0-7424-1822-7 *Problem Solving*

Name _____ Date _____

Estimating Will Do

There are times when we don't need the exact answer. An estimate that is close is okay. We use what we know. Then we make a guess.

1. Time yourself writing your name 10 times. How long does it take? _____

2. a. Now use your answer to guess how long it will take you to write your name 100 times. _____

    b. How did you make your guess? _____

3. Time yourself running around the room once.

    How long did it take? _____

4. Use this information. Guess how long it might take you to run around the room 5 times.

    Show your work. _____

5. Time yourself running around the gym 5 times.

    How long does it take? _____

    How close was your guess? _____

    Compare the estimate to the actual time. _____

Do More

Choose two activities. Estimate how long they will take. Then find the actual times.

0-7424-1822-7 *Problem Solving*

Name _____ Date _____

Length

Directions: Write **inches**, **feet**, or **yards** to complete each sentence. Choose the one that makes the most sense.

1. Mary's banana is 8 _____ long.

2. Paige's uncle is 6 _____ tall.

3. The maple tree is 4 _____ tall.

4. Li's book is 9 _____ long.

5. Jake's leash is 5 _____ long.

Directions: Name one thing that can be measured in inches, feet, and yards.

inches: _____   **feet:** _____

yards: _____

Do More

Find one more thing each to measure in inches, feet, and yards.

0-7424-1822-7 *Problem Solving*

Name _____ Date _____

How Long Are You?

Directions: Guess how big you are in inches and centimeters. Write your estimates below. Then have a friend use a ruler to measure. Write the actual length. How close were your estimates.

Height

Estimate _____   Estimate _____

Inches _____   Centimeters _____

Arm Length

Estimate _____   Estimate _____

Inches _____   Centimeters _____

Leg Length

Estimate _____   Estimate _____

Inches _____   Centimeters _____

Foot Length

Estimate _____   Estimate _____

Inches _____   Centimeters _____

Think

What does **estimate** mean?

0-7424-1822-7 *Problem Solving*

Name _____ Date _____

Let's Measure

You can measure with hands, feet, paper clips, and other objects. These are called **nonstandard** measurement tools. If you measure with a ruler in inches, feet, and yards, you are using **standard** measurement tools.

Directions: Measure and compare the length of objects using nonstandard and standard measurement tools.

	Paper Clips	**Inch Ruler**
length of desk top		
width of math book		
length of your leg		
length of your arm		

I. What did you find out about measuring with standard and nonstandard measurement tools?

_____

_____

2. Which was easier to do? Why?

_____

_____

Think

What might happen if we all measured with different nonstandard measurement tools?

72

0-7424-1822-7 *Problem Solving*

Name _____ Date _____

Following the Route

Directions: Look at the path Reuben took home. Measure each line and write the distance in meters. Then answer the questions. You may need to measure and draw lines to answer.

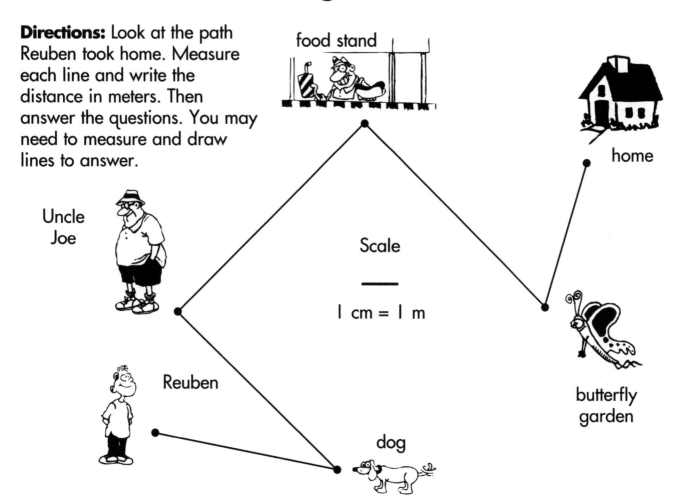

food stand

home

Uncle Joe

Scale

—

1 cm = 1 m

Reuben

butterfly garden

dog

1. How far did Reuben go in all? ____

2. If Reuben hadn't stopped at the food stand, how far would he have gone?

_____

3. Reuben's friend Claudia lives twice as far away as he walked. How far is that? _____

4. Draw the shortest way from Reuben to home. Label it in meters.

Do More

Explain one way you use length every day.

0-7424-1822-7 *Problem Solving*

Name _____ Date _____

Measuring Weight

Directions: Look at the table. Use it to answer the following questions. Show your work.

Object	Estimated Weight	Actual Weight
cup	16 grams	25 grams
washer	8 grams	6 grams
three balloons	18 grams	15 grams
two clips and washer	9 grams	14 grams
cup and water	40 grams	86 grams
balloon and air	8 grams	6 grams

1. What is the actual weight of 1 washer? Compare the actual to the estimated weight.

_____

2. What is the actual weight of 1 balloon? How did you find out?

_____

3. What would be the actual weight of 7 clips? How did you find out?

_____

Do More

Do this experiment in your class. Use a table to show what happens.

0-7424-1822-7 *Problem Solving*

Name _____ Date _____

Weighing

Directions: Look at each scale. Write the weight in kilograms.

1.

_____ kg

2.

_____ kg

3.

_____ kg

4. What do you notice about the number of socks and the amount of weight?

_____

_____

5. Draw a scale with socks that might show 5 kg.

Think

Where have you seen weight written? Why?

0-7424-1822-7 *Problem Solving*

Name _____ Date _____

It's a Matter of Weight

1 lb. = pound

1. A dog weighing 80 lb., a child weighing 60 lb., and a dad weighing 175 lb. wanted to go for a boat ride. The boat had a sticker on the seat that read "Boat Limit 350 lb." Was there going to be a problem? Explain why.

   _____

2. All the passengers on the boat need a life jacket, including the dog. Each life jacket will add another 8 lb. to the weight in the boat. Can they still go? How did you find your answer?

   _____

3. They absolutely must have a picnic lunch. It weighs 10 lb. Are they going to be able to eat on this boat trip?

   _____

Think

Where have you seen weight limits written? Why do you think they were there?

0-7424-1822-7 *Problem Solving*

Name _____ Date _____

At the Play

Directions: The drama club poured punch at the play. Use the drawings to help you answer the questions.

I cup

2 cups
I pint

2 pints
I quart

1. They poured 40 cups of punch. They gave away 36 cups. How much was left?

    I cup   I pint   I quart

2. One person drank I cup during the play. He came back for 3 more cups. How much did he drink in all?

    I pint   2 pints   2 quarts

3. You know you have I quart. How do you find how many cups you have? Show your work.

Do More

Fill actual cups with water to show the differences between cups, pints, and quarts.

      0-7424-1822-7 *Problem Solving*

Name _____ Date _____

Which One?

Directions: Volume is used to measure how much a container can hold. Volume can be measured in **cups**, **pints**, **quarts**, and **gallons**. Read each problem. Circle the best unit to use.

1. You are baking cookies. You measure the chocolate chips in…

    a. cups   **b.** pints   **c.** quarts   **d.** quarts

    How do you know? _____

2. You want to buy the largest container of milk you can. You buy a…

    a. quart   **b.** cup   **c.** pint   **d.** gallon

    How do you know? _____

3. You are filling a swimming pool. You will measure the water in…

    a. pints   **b.** cups   **c.** gallons   **d.** quarts

    How do you know? _____

4. You drink orange juice for breakfast. The closest measure to the amount you drink is…

    a. cup   **b.** quart   **c.** gallon   **d.** pints

    How do you know? _____

Do More

Think about how much food you eat each day. Do you have a cup of cereal for breakfast? Two cups of soda a day? Draw a dinner plate with portions of food. Write the number of cups of food on each item.

0-7424-1822-7 *Problem Solving*

Name _____ Date _____

Water Play

| 2 cups = 1 pint | 2 pints = 1 quart | 4 quarts = 1 gallon |

Directions: You will need at least 3 cup, pint, and quart containers and two 1-gallon containers. You will also need lots of water. Place all your containers in line from smallest to largest. First estimate and then measure to check.

1. How many cups do you think it will take to fill 1 pint?

       Estimate: _____   Measure: _____

2. How many cups do you think it takes to fill 3 pints?

       Estimate: _____   Measure: _____

3. How many quarts does it take to fill 2 gallons?

       Estimate: _____   Measure: _____

4. How many pints does it take to fill 3 quarts?

       Estimate: _____   Measure: _____

5. How many pints does it take to fill 1 gallon?

       Estimate: _____   Measure: _____

Think

How do you use your measuring skills to help you outside of school?

0-7424-1822-7 *Problem Solving*

Name _____ Date _____

Area

Directions: Look at each rectangle. Find the area. The first one is done for you.

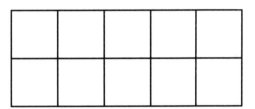

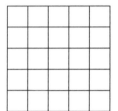

1. _____10 square units_____   2. _____

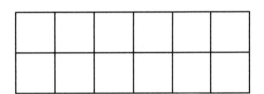

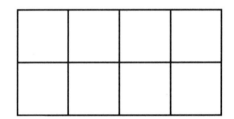

3. _____   4. _____

5. Draw a square that has an area of 36 square units.

6. Draw a rectangle that has an area of 18 square units.

Do More

Use grid paper to find the area of building blocks. Lay a building block on grid paper. Trace around it. Lift up the block and count the square units to find the area.

0-7424-1822-7 *Problem Solving*

Name _____ Date _____

Square Units

Directions: Area is the space that something covers. Count the squares in the shaded shapes to find the area of each. Write the number on the line.

1.

_____ square units

2.

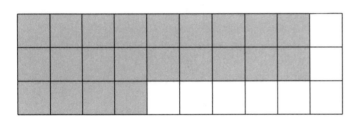

_____ square units

Directions: Draw shapes with the number of square units shown.

3.

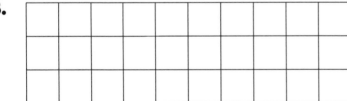

12 square units

4.

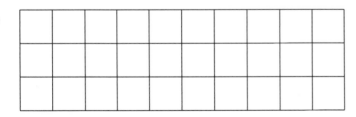

25 square units

Think

How can you use area in your classroom?

0-7424-1822-7 *Problem Solving*

Name _____ Date _____

A Little Help Goes a Long Way

Melissa (who is 4) and Ryan (who is 7) need to help their dad. He wants to move small bricks from the front of the house to the back. Melissa is little and can carry only 1 brick at a time. It took her about 3 minutes to carry 1 brick and go back. She moved 10 bricks before she went off to play.

1. How many minutes did it take her to move the 10 bricks? _____

2. How did you find your answer? _____

Ryan bragged that he could carry 2 bricks each time. However, he liked to play while he worked. It took him about 4 minutes to move 2 bricks and go back. He quit working after he had moved 20 bricks.

3. How long did it take Ryan to move 20 bricks? _____

Dad used a special brick carrier and could carry 10 bricks at a time. He worked for 120 minutes. He moved 300 bricks in 30 trips to the backyard.

4. How many minutes did it take Dad to make 1 trip? _____

5. What steps did you take to find out the answer? _____

_____

Do More

Place a pile of wooden blocks at one end of the room. Time how long each student takes to move all the bricks to the other side of the room. Move bricks one at a time. Create a bar graph to show the results of the whole class.

82

0-7424-1822-7 *Problem Solving*

Name _____ Date _____

Winter Work

Jasmyn and Kieran shovel snow from sidewalks to earn money in the wintertime. It takes them $\frac{1}{2}$ hour to shovel a sidewalk together.

1. How many minutes are there in $\frac{1}{2}$ hour? _____

2. How many sidewalks can Jasmyn and Kieran shovel in 4 hours? _____

Show how you found your answer.

3. **a.** If they get home from school at 3:30 and shovel 4 sidewalks before dinner, what time will they be finished? _____

b. How do you know your answer is correct? _____

c. Draw two clocks to show the time they start and finish.

4. Jasmyn and Kieran shovel a total of 14 sidewalks in 1 week.

a. How many minutes do they spend working in all? _____

b. Change the minutes into hours. How many hours did they work? _____

Think

What do you do each day where time is important?

0-7424-1822-7 *Problem Solving*

Name _____ Date _____

Create Your Own Problems

1. Draw 3 groups of 3 objects. Have a classmate order them by length.

2. Draw a map from your house to school where inches equal miles. Write questions to go with your map.

3. Write a story that talks about weight. It could be set at the grocery store, the doctor's office, or at a home. Write questions about your story.

4. Draw a shape that is a certain number of square units. Do not draw the squares on the shape. Challenge a classmate to find the area.

0-7424-1822-7 *Problem Solving*

Name _____ Date _____

Check Your Skills

1. Choose the best unit (inch, foot, or yard) to measure the following.

   a. book cover _____

   b. running track _____

   c. your height _____

2. Look at the chart. Answer the questions.

Objects	Weight
2 pencils	10 grams
paper	1 gram
scissor	15 grams

   a. How much more does the scissor weigh than the piece of paper? _____

   b. How much does 1 pencil weigh? _____

   How do you know? _____

3. You have 2 cups. How many pints do you have? _____

4. Aunt Marcie drank a gallon of punch. How many cups did she drink? _____

0-7424-1822-7 *Problem Solving*

Name _____ Date _____

Check Your Skills (cont.)

5. Find the area of each shape below. Write it in square units.

a. 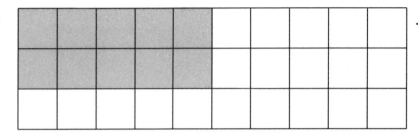 _____

b. 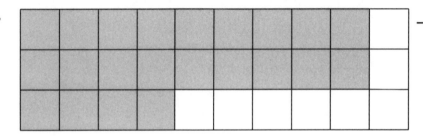 _____

6. Draw a shape that is 13 square units.

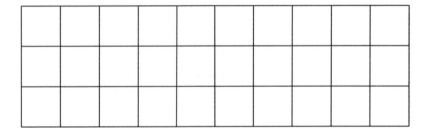

7. Dena spends $\frac{1}{2}$ hour in the bathroom getting ready for the party. How many minutes does she spend in the bathroom? _____

8. Dena spends another $\frac{1}{2}$ hour deciding what to wear and 15 minutes getting dressed. How many minutes does Dena take to get ready (include your answer from #7)? _____

0-7424-1822-7 *Problem Solving*

Name _____ Date _____

Sort and Graph

Use with page 88.

Directions: Look at the animals in the box. Think about how they are alike. Then count the animals and fill in the graph on page 88. Look carefully at the describing words.

0-7424-1822-7 *Problem Solving*

Name _____ Date _____

Sort and Graph (cont.)

Use with page 87.

6					
5					
4					
3					
2					
1					
Mammals	Birds	Fish	Insects	Reptiles	Amphibians

Think

How did you know how to sort?

0-7424-1822-7 *Problem Solving*

Name _____ Date _____

Where Does It Belong?

Directions: Write each word in the correct row below.

boat   carrot   van   book

plane   glue   pie   desk   turkey

1. Things we eat:

_____   _____   _____

2. Things we ride in:

_____   _____   _____

3. Things at school:

_____   _____   _____

Directions: Now write three things that go below.

4. Things we listen to:

_____   _____   _____

Do More

Write how you knew what to put in each group.

    0-7424-1822-7 *Problem Solving*

Name _____ Date _____

Venn Diagram

Directions: Read the paragraph. Use the Venn diagram to sort. Answer the questions.

There are 18 dogs.
Nine dogs like to eat Puppy Tracks.
Fifteen dogs like to eat Diggidy Dog.
Six dogs like to eat both Puppy Tracks and Diggidy Dog.

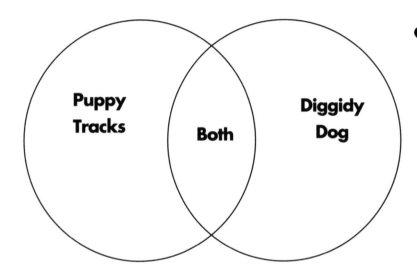

Puppy Tracks   **Both**   **Diggidy Dog**

1. How many dogs like only Puppy Tracks? _____

2. How many dogs like only Diggidy Dog? _____

3. How many dogs like both? _____

Think

What math operations did you use to fill in each section of the diagram?

0-7424-1822-7 *Problem Solving*

Name _____ Date _____

? ? ? *Ask Questions* ? ? ?

Directions: Look at each topic below. Write one question about each topic. Then take a survey to find answers for each question. How would you display the results? Make a bar graph? Make a pictograph? The first one has been done for you.

1. School Lunches

Question: What is the favorite school lunch in our school?

How: Take a survey of students from each grade. Make a bar graph.

2. Playground

Question: _____

How: _____

3. Transportation

Question: _____

How: _____

4. Sports

Question: _____

How: _____

Think

Where have you seen a survey? What was the question? Why do you think it was being asked?

?
?
?
?
?

91

0-7424-1822-7 *Problem Solving*

Name _____ Date _____

Survey Questions

Directions: Look at each picture. Write two questions about each picture. The questions must be able to be answered by taking a survey. A survey is when people are asked their opinions.

1. _____
   _____
   _____
   _____

2. _____
   _____
   _____
   _____

3. _____
   _____
   _____
   _____

4. _____
   _____
   _____
   _____

Do More

Take one of your questions and conduct a survey. Create a pictograph to show your results.

0-7424-1822-7 *Problem Solving*

Name _____ Date _____

Representing Data

Directions: Look at the data. Fill in the bar graph.

At Sweets and Treats ice cream shop,
the number of ice cream cones sold
each month was:

January—50	July—225
February—50	August—250
March—75	September—225
April—75	October—125
May—125	November—75
June—175	December—50

Ice Cream Sold per Month

	Jan.	Feb.	Mar.	Apr.	May	June	July	Aug.	Sept.	Oct.	Nov.	Dec.
250												
225												
200												
175												
125												
100												
75												
50												
25												

Ice Cream Cones / **Months of the Year**

Think

Do you see a pattern in the graph? Tell why you think this might be.

0-7424-1822-7 *Problem Solving*

Name _____ Date _____

Representing Data in Different Ways

Directions: Look at the tally chart. Use the data to fill in the bar graph and the pictograph. Make sure the data you show is the same.

Tally Chart

Grade Level	Library Hours
First	I
Second	I I
Third	I I I I I
Fourth	I I
Fifth	⊦⊦⊦⊦

Time in the Library

= I hour

Pictograph

Time in the Library

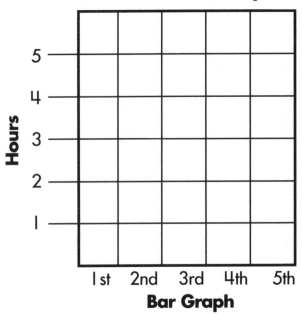

Hours: 5, 4, 3, 2, I

1st 2nd 3rd 4th 5th

Bar Graph

Think

Which graph is easier to read and understand?

0-7424-1822-7 *Problem Solving*

Name _____ Date _____

Show It Twice

Directions: Read the data in the pie graph about Summer Fun Camp. Use the data to make a bar graph.

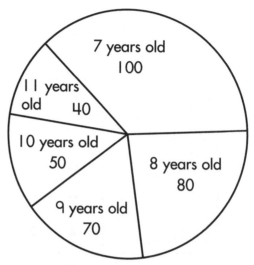

Number of Students by Age at Summer Fun Camp

100					
90					
80					
70					
60					
50					
40					
30					
20					
10					
Number of Students	7	8	9	10	11
	Ages at Summer Fun Camp				

Think

What do you notice about the number of students and their ages?

0-7424-1822-7 *Problem Solving*

Name _____ Date _____

What Does It Mean?

Directions: Look at the pictograph. Answer the questions about what it means.

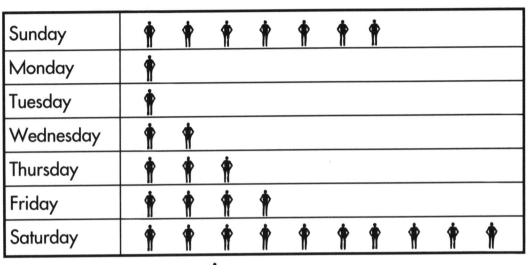

🕯 = 5 students

1. How many students went to the mall this week in all? _____

2. How many more students went on Friday than on Thursday? _____

3. On which day were the most students at the mall? _____

4. Why do you think more students went on Saturday?

_____

Think

How could the information on the graph be useful to the people who own the mall?

0-7424-1822-7 *Problem Solving*

Name _____ Date _____

Describing It

Directions: Look at the graph. Answer the questions.

1. Write one sentence telling the difference between two weeks in January.

_____

_____

2. Write one sentence that tells about the weather overall in December.

_____

_____

3. Write two questions that could be answered by looking at this graph.

_____

_____

Snowy Days in December

Week 1	❄ ❄ ❄ ❄
Week 2	❄ ❄ ❄
Week 3	❄ ❄ ❄ ❄ ❄ ❄
Week 4	❄ ❄ ❄ ❄

❄ = 2 days

Do More

Create a bar graph using the information in the pictograph.

97

Name _____ Date _____

Let's Investigate

Use with pages 99–100.

Directions: Survey your classmates by asking these questions. Use tally marks to record each **yes** answer. Do not record the **no** answers. Then fill in the bar graph on page 99. After you fill in bar graph, answer the questions on page 100.

1. Do you like pizza?

2. Do you have a pet?

3. Do you know how to swim?

4. Can you whistle?

5. Do you like to dance?

0-7424-1822-7 *Problem Solving*

Name _____ Date _____

Let's Investigate (cont.)

Use with pages 98 and 100.

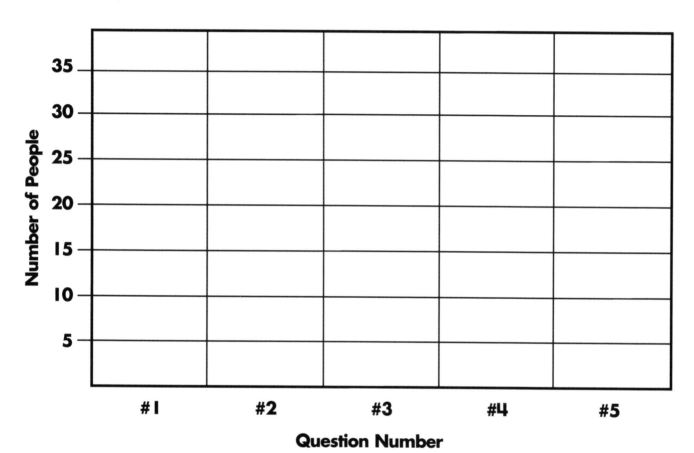

0-7424-1822-7 *Problem Solving*

Name _____ Date _____

Let's Investigate (cont.)

Use with pages 98–99.

1. a. Which question received the most "yes" answers? _____

b. Why do you suppose so many people were able to answer "yes" to this question?

_____

_____

_____

_____

2. a. Look at the results from question 2. How many of your classmates do not have a pet? _____

b. How were you able to find this answer?

_____

_____

_____

_____

Do More

Describe what you learned from working with this survey. On the back of this paper, list at least 10 facts you can find from reading your graph.

0-7424-1822-7 *Problem Solving*

Name _____ Date _____

Likely/Unlikely

Directions: Read each sentence. Is it likely or unlikely? "Likely" means it will probably happen. "Unlikely" means it probably won't.

1. There are big black clouds. It will rain.

    LIKELY   UNLIKELY

2. You have a baby. You hear crying.

    LIKELY   UNLIKELY

3. Your family likes pizza. They will eat it often.

    LIKELY   UNLIKELY

4. You are wearing a baseball uniform. You are going to play football.

    LIKELY   UNLIKELY

5. You are sneezing. You must go to the hospital.

    LIKELY   UNLIKELY

6. Write one thing that is likely to happen. Why?

    _____

7. Write on thing that is unlikely to happen. Why?

    _____

Think

How do you know if something is likely or unlikely?

0-7424-1822-7 *Problem Solving*

Name _____ Date _____

Possibilities

Directions: Something that can happen is **possible**. Something that cannot happen is **impossible**. Circle possible or impossible for each situation.

1. 6 = 15

   possible   **impossible**

   Write why. _____

2. 8 doubled is 16

   possible   **impossible**

3. You roll 2 dice and get a sum of 55.

   possible   **impossible**

4.

   possible   **impossible**

5.

   possible   **impossible**

   Write why. _____

Do More

Explain what is meant by **possible** and **impossible**.

102

        0-7424-1822-7 *Problem Solving*

Name _____ Date _____

Create Your Own Problems

1. Create a bar graph. Make up results from a survey about favorite foods. Write four questions about the graph.

   a. _____

   b. _____

   c. _____

   d. _____

2. Think of two topics that interest you. Write one question for each.

   a. _____

   b. _____

3. Write one sentence that is **likely** and one that is **unlikely**.

   _____

   _____

   _____

0-7424-1822-7 *Problem Solving*

Name _____ Date _____

Check Your Skills

1. Write each animal word in the correct box.

worm   kangaroo   bee   cow   whale   bear   fly   mouse

Big Animals	Small Animals

2. Write one survey question for each topic.

a. jobs

_____

b. food

_____

3. Use the information below. Make a pictograph.

Scout Cookies Sold (boxes)
Monday—10
Tuesday—7
Wednesday—6
Thursday—8
Friday—9
Saturday—12
Sunday—6

0-7424-1822-7 *Problem Solving*

Name _____ Date _____

Check Your Skills (cont.)

4. Look at the tally chart. Show the data as a bar graph.

Grade Level	Computer Lab Hours
First	ΙΙ
Second	₩
Third	ΙΙ
Fourth	ΙΙΙΙ
Fifth	ΙΙ

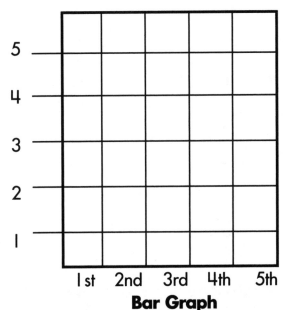

Bar Graph

5. Circle **possible** or **impossible**.

a. $12 = 3 + 4$

possible   **impossible**

b. Rolling two dice and getting a sum of 24.

possible   **impossible**

c. a flying carpet

possible   **impossible**

d. getting lost on a car trip

possible   **impossible**

    0-7424-1822-7 *Problem Solving*

Name _____ Date _____

Cumulative Post Test

1. Write the largest number you can make with the numerals 1, 4, 2, and 9.

_____

2. Round these numbers to the nearest ten.

   a. 26 _____

   b. 55 _____

   c. 17 _____

3. Round these numbers to the nearest hundred.

   a. 168 _____

   b. 152 _____

   c. 170 _____

4. Sherry ate $\frac{1}{4}$ of a pie. Draw the pie.
Divide it into the correct number of pieces.
Color the part of the pie Sherry ate.

5. Fill in the chart. Write the rule.

IN	1	2	3	4	5
OUT	21	22	23		

Rule: _____

© McGraw-Hill Children's Publishing   0-7424-1822-7 *Problem Solving*

Cumulative Post Test (cont.)

6. Draw a line of symmetry on the shapes below.

7. Which is larger—3 pints or 1 quart? How do you know?

_____

8. Draw a rectangle with an area of 14 square units.

9. Use this information to make a bar graph.

Amount of Rain (inches)
Week 1—7 inches
Week 2—4 inches
Week 3—2 inches
Week 4—1 inch

10. What is one pattern you notice about your graph?

_____

0-7424-1822-7 Problem Solving

Tangrams

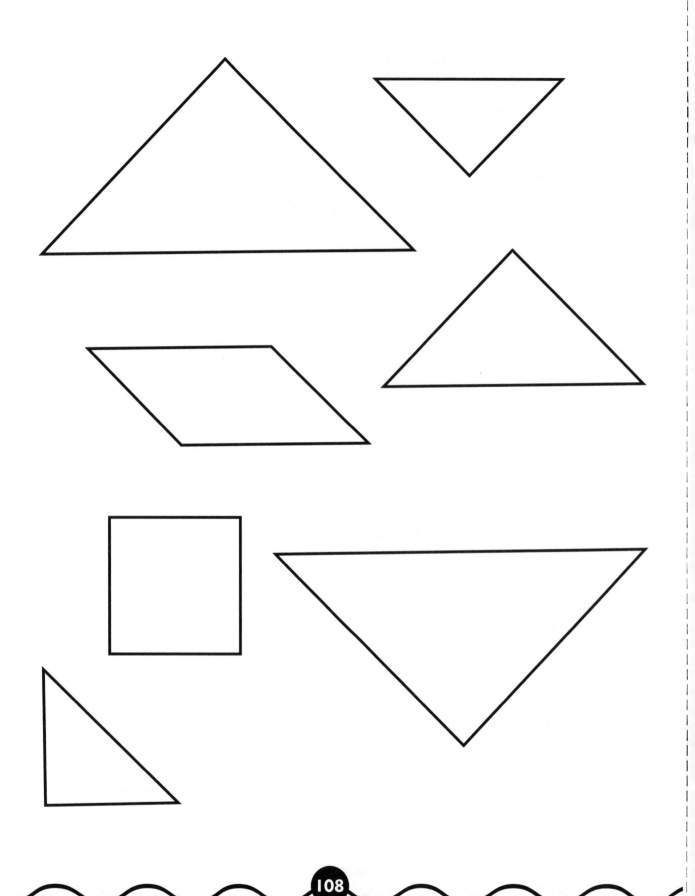

0-7424-1822-7 *Problem Solving*

Pentominoes

0-7424-1822-7 *Problem Solving*

Hundred Chart

1	2	3	4	5	6	7	8	9	10
11	12	13	14	15	16	17	18	19	20
21	22	23	24	25	26	27	28	29	30
31	32	33	34	35	36	37	38	39	40
41	42	43	44	45	46	47	48	49	50
51	52	53	54	55	56	57	58	59	60
61	62	63	64	65	66	67	68	69	70
71	72	73	74	75	76	77	78	79	80
81	82	83	84	85	86	87	88	89	90
91	92	93	94	95	96	97	98	99	100

0-7424-1822-7 *Problem Solving*

Answer Key

Problem-Solving Challenge **7–8**

1. $5,000 + 200 + 30 + 4$

2. **a.** $22 + 2 = 24$

   b. $26 - 2 = 24$

   c. $12 + 12 = 24$

3. $\frac{1}{4}$

4–5. Answers will vary.

6. **a.** feet

   b. inches

   c. yards

7. Pictograph should reflect data shown.
   The number of 100% tests increases.

Place Value **9**

1. $600.00; six hundred dollars

2. **a.** 71 years old

   b. $70 + 1$

   c. Answers will vary.

3. **a.** 9,521

   b. $9,000 + 500 + 20 + 1$

   c. nine thousand, five hundred twenty-one

Number Combinations **10**

1. Answers will vary.

2. 9,531

3. 3,579

Rounding Numbers **11–12**

1. **a.** 130

   b. 50

   c. 70

   d. 80

   e. 20

   f. 70

   g. 40

   h. 30

2. **a.** 100

   b. 100

   c. 200

   d. 800

   e. 500

   f. 300

   g. 300

   h. 400

3. $20.00; $17.00; $39.00; $10.00

4. $86.00; $85.85; $0.15

5. $40.00

6. $9.16; $9.00

7. $49.00

8. $48.91

9. Buying is $37.00 more.

10. Answers will vary.

Putting Numbers Together **13**

1. 6 combinations; 358, 385, 538, 583, 835, 853

2. 6 ways

3–4. Answers will vary.

Adding Odd and Even **14**

1. **a.** 10; 86; 76; 3,546

   b. even

2. **a.** 660; 32; 100; 6,134

   b. even

3. **a.** 67; 33; 571; 1,175

   b. odd

Subtracting Odd and Even **15**

1. even, 2, 6, 6, 1,108

2. even, 2, 6, 122, 1,620

3. odd, 5, 25, 137, 1,355

4. Answers will vary.

0-7424-1822-7 *Problem Solving*

Answer Key (cont.)

Fractions 16

1. $\frac{1}{2}$

2. $\frac{1}{4}$

3. $\frac{1}{2}$

4. Answers will vary.

5. $\frac{1}{2}$

Fraction Bars 17

1. whole

2. $\frac{1}{2}$

3. 3; $\frac{1}{3}$

4. 4; $\frac{1}{4}$

5. a. $\frac{1}{3}$

   b. $\frac{1}{2}$

   c. $\frac{1}{2}$

Choose Your Operation 18

1. a. +; +

   b. + ; +

   c. −; +

   d. − ; +

2–3. Answers will vary.

Missing Numbers 19

Answers may vary. Sample answers are:

1. a. $8 + 4 = 12$

   b. $18 - 4 = 14$

   c. $8 + 9 + 9 = 26$

   d. $16 - 10 + 3 = 9$

   e. $10 + 4 = 4 + 10$

   f. $10 + 10 = 22 - 2$

2–3. Answers will vary.

Groups and Pairs 20

1. 10

2–3. Answers will vary.

Calendar Calculations 21

1. 70 days, x

2. 364 weeks

3. 1,825 days

Find the Sums 22

Answers will vary.

Making Change 23

1. $0.55

2. $2.10

3. $0.90

Divide It Up 24

1. $\frac{1}{2}$ sandwich, 12 grapes, 3 cookies, $\frac{1}{2}$ carton of milk

2. a. 18 chickens

   b. 18 horses

   c. Answers will vary

0-7424-1822-7 *Problem Solving*

Answer Key (cont.)

5-Step Problem Solving **25–26**

Problem 1

Step 1: How many goals did Ken score?

Step 2: number of boys on team; ages; uniform color

Step 3: 18 goals—Sept.; 23 goals—Oct.;
25 goals—Nov.

Step 4: in all means +

Step 5: 66 goals

Problem 2

Step 1: How many crayons in the box?

Step 2: age; grade; number of students

Step 3: 1 crayon for day each of 6 months

Step 4: how many means +

Step 5: 62 crayons

Create Your Own Problems **27**

Answers will vary.

Check Your Skills **28–29**

1. 3,000 + 500 + 90 + 8; three thousand, five hundred ninety-eight

2. Divide 3,598 by 2.

3. 9,831

4. **a.** 24 + 6 = 40 − 10
   b. 6 − 6 + 6 = 3 + 2 + 1

5–6. Answers will vary.

7. $\frac{1}{4}$

8. **a.** $4.00
   b. $0.41

9. $6.00

Predicting Patterns **30**

Patterns should be continued.

Mosaic Tiles **31**

Answers will vary.

One Hundred Chart **32**

1. **a.** Check coloring.
   b. Answers will vary.
   c. 50; all even numbers 2–100

2. **a.** Check coloring.
   b. 16
   c. 99

3. 3

Patterns with Letters and Numbers **33**

1. letter, number in progressive order

2. I9, J10, K11, L12, M13, N14, O15, P16, Q17, R18, S19, T20, U21, V22, W23, X24, Y25, Z26

3. Answers will vary.

Flag Patterns **34**

Answers will vary. Sample answers are: Strips alternate red and white, Stars in rows of 6, 5, 6, 5, etc.

Recognizing Patterns **35**

1. 5, 6, 7; Rule: + 2

2. 8, 9, 10; Rule: + 5

3. 4, 3, 2; Rule: − 3

Addition and Subtraction with Symbols . . **36**

1. 15

2. 14

3. 23

4. 19

5. Answers will vary.

0-7424-1822-7 *Problem Solving*

Answer Key (cont.)

Modeling with Symbols 37

1. 26

2. 23

3. 11

4. 16

Using Comparison Signs 38

1. >

2. <

3. <

4. <

5. <

6. greater than

7. less than

8. equal to

9. Answers will vary.

Symbolic Notation 39

1. <; 34 is less than 47.

2. >; 98 is greater than 89.

3. >; 10 is greater than 7.

4. =; 54 is equal to 54.

5. >; 298 is greater than 297.

6. <; 67 is less than 75.

7. <; 18 is less than 27.

8. >; 143 is greater than 134.

Properties of Operations 40

1. 12

2. 6

3. 6

4. 4

5. 9

6. 10

7–10. Answers will vary.

Working with Zero 41

1. a. 9

b. 9

c. 21

d. 21

2. The sum is the same as the other number.

3. It doesn't change the sum.

4. a. 16

b. no

c. 99

d. no

e. 12

f. no

5. The difference is the same as the other number.

6. You can't invert a subtraction problem using all positive numbers.

Qualitative Change 42

1. b

2. a

3. shorter; cut off

4. bigger; he weighs more

Quantitative Change 43

1. higher

2. Answers may vary. Between Oct. and Nov. or between Mar. and Apr. are acceptable answers.

3. Answers will vary.

Create Some Order 44

1. a. Christen, Tommy, Zed

b. Christen, Zed, Tommy

0-7424-1822-7 *Problem Solving*

Answer Key (cont.)

Order It 45
 1. Robert—vacuum
    Karen—dishes
    Mike—books
 2. Answers will vary.
 3. ages

Create Your Own Problems 46
 Answers will vary.

Check Your Skills 47–48
 1. ABCD
 2. letter, number in progressive order
 3. **a.** 3, 4; minus 1
    b. 8, 10; double the number
    c. 14, 15; add 10
 4. 15 − 4 = 11
 5. **a.** greater than
    b. less than
    c. equal to
 6. **a.** >
    b. =
    c. =
    d. >
 7. **a.** 0
    b. 45
    c. 51

Fit It Together 49
 Answers will vary.

Building 2-D Shapes 50
 1. circle
 2. pentagon
 3. octagon
 4. triangle
 5. square
 6. hexagon
 7. rectangle
 8. Answers will vary.

3-D Shapes 51
 1. cube
 2. cone
 3. cylinder
 4. prism
 5. sphere
 6–7. Answers will vary.

What Am I? 52
 1. triangle
 2. cylinder
 3. cube
 4. rectangle

Compare and Order 53
 1. 1, 3, 2
 2. 1, 2, 3
 3. 2, 1, 3
 4–5. Answers will vary.

Group Them. 54
 Group 1: even number of sides
 Group 2: odd number of sides

© McGraw-Hill Children's Publishing

0-7424-1822-7 *Problem Solving*

Answer Key (cont.)

Same Size, Same Shape **55**

  I. a. true

    b. false

    c. true

  2. They are not exactly the same size.

  3. Answers will vary.

Symmetrical Shapes **56**

  I. yes

  2. no

  3. yes

  4. yes

  5. no

  6. Answers will vary.

Complete the Shapes **57**

All shapes should be symmetrical.

Slides, Flips, Turns **58**

  I. b

  2. a

  3. c

4–6. Answers will vary.

Finding Perimeter **61**

  I. 7 in.; 12 cm

  2. All the sides are the same; 12 cm

  3. a rectangle with two sides labeled 2 in. and two sides labeled 3 in.

Position and Location **62**

  I. swimming pool

  2. 4 mi.

  3. ice cream shop, swimming pool, petting zoo

  4. Answers will vary.

Coordinates **63**

  I. (2, 5)

  2. B

  3. star drawn at (5, 1)

Using Coordinate Grids **64**

The drawing is a car.

Create Your Own Problems **65**

Answers will vary.

Check Your Skills **66–67**

  I. a. circle

    b. square

    c. rectangle

    d. triangle

    e. pentagon

    f. hexagon

    g. octagon

  2. a. cylinder

    b. sphere

    c. prism

    d. cube

    e. cone

  3. cube

  4. the same on both sides

  5. exactly the same size and shape

  6. Answers will vary.

  7. A; box drawn at (4, 3)

In Order **68**

Estimates will vary.

Estimating Will Do **69**

Answers will vary.

0-7424-1822-7 *Problem Solving*

Answer Key (cont.)

Length **70**

1. inches
2. feet
3. yards
4. inches
5. feet

How Long Are You? **71**

Answers will vary.

Let's Measure **72**

Answers will vary.

Following the Route **73**

1. 29 m
2. 25 m
3. 58 m
4. 14 m

Measuring Weight **74**

1. 6 g; 2 g less
2. 5 g; divide weight of 3 balloons by 3
3. 28 g; Subtract washer from "two clips and washer." Then divide by 2. Multiply by 7.

Weighing **75**

1. 3 kg
2. 4 kg
3. 2 kg
4. As the number of socks increases, so does the weight.
5. Scale should show more socks than in number 2.

It's a Matter of Weight **76**

1. No; They weigh 315 lb., and the limit on the boat is 350 lb.
2. They can still go; Add 8 lb. three times to 315 lb.
3. They can take a lunch; The boat will weigh 349 lb.

At the Play **77**

1. 1 quart
2. 2 pints
3. 1 quart = 2 pints
   1 pint = 2 cups
   2 pints = 4 cups

Which One? **78**

1. a
2. d
3. c
4. a

Water Play **79**

1. 2
2. 6
3. 8
4. 6
5. 8

Area **80**

1. 10 square units
2. 25 square units
3. 12 square units
4. 8 square units

0-7424-1822-7 *Problem Solving*

Answer Key (cont.)

Square Units **81**

1. 10 square units

2. 22 square units

3. Shape should have 12 square units.

4. Shape should have 25 square units.

A Little Help Goes a Long Way **82**

1. 30 min.

2. Add 3 min. ten times or multiply 3 by 10.

3. 40 min.

4. 4 min.

5. Divide the total time by the number of trips.

Winter Work **83**

1. 30 min.

2. 8 sidewalks

3. 5:30

4. **a.** 420 min.

   b. 7 hours

Create Your Own Problems **84**

Answers will vary.

Check Your Skills **85–86**

1. **a.** inches

   b. yards

   c. feet

2. **a.** 14 grams

   b. 5 grams; divide 10 by 2

3. 1 pint

4. 16 cups

5. **a.** 10 square units

   b. 22 square units

6. Shape should be 13 square units.

7. 30 min.

8. 1 hr. 15 min.

Sort and Graph **87–88**

Mammals—3

Birds—2

Fish—2

Insects—3

Reptiles—3

Amphibians—1

Where Does It Belong? **89**

1. carrot, pie, turkey

2. boat, van, plane

3. book, glue, desk

4. Answers will vary.

Venn Diagram **90**

1. 3 dogs

2. 9 dogs

3. 6 dogs

0-7424-1822-7 *Problem Solving*

Answer Key (cont.)

Ask Questions 91

Answers will vary.

Survey Questions 92

Answers will vary.

Representing Data 93

January—50

February—50

March—75

April—75

May—125

June—175

July—225

August—250

September—225

October—125

November—75

December—50

Representing Data in Different Ways 94

Graphs should show:

1st—1

2nd—2

3rd—4

4th—2

5th—5

Show It Twice 95

Graph should show:

7—100

8—80

9—70

10—50

11—40

What Does It Mean? 96

1. 140 students

2. 5 more

3. Saturday

4. They had more time to go on the weekend

Describing It 97

Answers will vary.

Let's Investigate 98–100

Answers will vary.

Likely/Unlikely 101

1. likely

2. likely

3. likely

4. unlikely

5. unlikely

6–7. Answers will vary.

© McGraw-Hill Children's Publishing

0-7424-1822-7 *Problem Solving*

Answer Key (cont.)

Possibilities 102

1. impossible
2. possible
3. impossible
4. possible
5. impossible

Create Your Own Problems 103

Answers will vary.

Check Your Skills 104–105

1. Big—kangaroo, cow, whale, bear
   Small—worm, bee, fly, mouse
2. Answers will vary.
3. The information should be shown in a pictograph.
4. The bar graph should reflect the tally chart.
5. a. impossible
   b. impossible
   c. impossible
   d. possible

Cumulative Post Test 106–107

1. 9,421
2. a. 30
   b. 60
   c. 20
3. a. 200
   b. 200
   c. 200
4. $\frac{1}{4}$ pie should be colored.
5. 24, 25; add 20
6. Correct lines of symmetry should be drawn.
7. 3 pints; 3 pints = 6 cups and 1 quart = 4 cups
8. A rectangle of 14 square units should be drawn.
9. Bar graph should reflect information shown.
10. The amount of rain decreases.

© McGraw-Hill Children's Publishing

0-7424-1822-7 *Problem Solving*

congruent	**similar**
symmetry	**line of symmetry**
estimate	**sum**

0-7424-1822-7 *Problem Solving*

objects that are
the same shape
but not
the same size

objects that are
exactly the same
size and shape

a line that
divides a shape
so each side is
symmetrical

when one side of
a shape is the
mirror image of
the other side

the answer to an
addition problem

a good guess
based on what
you know

0-7424-1822-7 Problem Solving

area	volume
3-D	**2-D**
likely	unlikely

0-7424-1822-7 *Problem Solving*

the amount
a container
can hold

the space inside
a 2-dimensional
shape

a flat shape

a shape
that has
width, length,
and height

probably
won't happen

probably
will happen

0-7424-1822-7 *Problem Solving*

standard form	**expanded form**
written form	**equation**
operation	**tally marks**

0-7424-1822-7 *Problem Solving*

a number written with all of its place values broken up

ex:
123 = 100 + 20 + 3

a number written with numerals

ex: 123

a number sentence with an equal (=) sign

a number written out in words

ex: one hundred twenty-three

sets of lines drawn to show how many

꘡꘡꘡꘡

a math sign that shows you what to do

ex: +, −, x, ÷, <, >, =

0-7424-1822-7 *Problem Solving*

survey

double

data/
information

slide

flip

turn

0-7424-1822-7 *Problem Solving*

two times
a number

a number twice

to ask people
what they think

to move a shape
without flipping
or turning

things you know
or learn about
something

to rotate a shape

to turn over
a shape

0-7424-1822-7 *Problem Solving*